World of Faiths

Judaism

Angela Gluck Wood

QEB Publishing

For B'ni,
son of my right hand

First published in the United States by
QEB Publishing, Inc.
23062 La Cadena Drive
Laguna Hills, CA 92653

www.qeb-publishing.com

Library of Congress Control Number:
2005911043

ISBN 978-1-59566-209-5

Written by Angela Gluck Wood
Designed by Tall Tree Books
Editor Louisa Somerville
Consultant John Keast
Illustrations by Laure Fournier

Publisher Steve Evans
Creative Director Zeta Davies
Editorial Director Jean Coppendale

Printed and bound in China

Picture credits
Key: t = top, b = bottom, c = center, l = left, r = right, FC = front cover

Alamy/Israel images Richard Nowitz 5tr/ Rafi Rondel 4/ Israel images Karen Benzian 20;
Ark Religion/John Arnold 27b/ Ask Images 12/ Rafael Ben-ari 14/ Itzhak Genut 10, 11t,
18, 21t&b, 22tr/ Hanan Isachar 22b/ Ken Mclaren 24/ Juliette Soester 15t/ Adina Tovy 25t;
Corbis/ Najlah Feanny 8/ Mark Kratsman 23b/ Richard T Nowitz 5b, 13l/ Mark Peterson
13t/ David H Wells 19; **Getty images**/Bushnell/Sulfer FC/ Lawrence Migdale 17tr/
All other images kindly supplied by the author.

Words in **bold** are explained
in the glossary on page 30.

Contents

What is Judaism?

Judaism is the religion of the Jewish people who first lived in the **Middle East**, in and near the land of present-day Israel, about 4,000 years ago. Being Jewish means being part of a tradition thousands of years old and feeling part of a worldwide family.

▼ A market stand selling four special plants that are used during the Jewish festival of Sukkot (see page 14).

A change of name

At first, the Jews were called **Hebrews**, which means "crossed over," because they crossed over from believing in many gods and worshipping statues to believing in one God. Later they were called **Israelites**, which means the ones who "struggle with God," and finally they were called Jews, which means "praising God." Hebrew remains the name given to the language of Jewish religious writings and prayers. Hebrew is also the everyday language used in Israel.

Jews worldwide

Today there are about 13 million Jews who live in many parts of the world. About five million Jews live in Israel, and nearly as many live in the U.S. Until the 20th century, there were also large communities in Eastern Europe and Arab countries.

▲ A family eating a special supper, called a seder, at the Jewish festival of Passover.

Jewish symbols

The oldest Jewish symbol is a seven-branched candlestick called a menorah. There was a large menorah in the ancient temple in **Jerusalem**. It was a symbol of the presence of God. Another important symbol is the Shield (or Star) of David. Today the Shield of David is part of the flag of Israel.

▲ A picture of a menorah in a stained-glass window.

What do Jews believe?

Jews believe in one God, who is a spirit rather than having a human form. They believe that God made a "brit" with them—a promise to belong to each other. In Judaism, believing is important and belonging is important, but the most important thing is behaving.

Journey to freedom

The descendants of Abraham (see page 22) were forced through famine to move to Egypt, where they were slaves for 400 years. The pharaohs (leaders) made them work long and hard, and often beat them. Jews believe that God told a man named Moses to lead them to a land of their own.

The escape from Egypt

Moses said to Pharaoh, "Let my people go." But Pharaoh refused.

So God sent ten plagues of terrible things, such as locusts, to Pharaoh's people. Pharaoh thought that he was being punished and he finally said, "Go!" The Jews quickly baked bread for the journey and left at night. They walked for seven days until they came to the Sea of Reeds.

There was a dry path across the sea. Again the Jews felt that God had helped them. On the other side, women led the singing and danced for joy.

In the wilderness

Ahead lay a wilderness that would take 40 years to cross. The Jews lived in sukkot (temporary shelters) that they made from whatever they could find. In the wilderness, God gave Moses the Torah—the Jews' teaching for life. Part of the Torah is **The Ten Sayings**. These are commandments, or rules, for Jewish life.

Now the Jews were ready for a new life in a place on the other side of the wilderness—a place they called the Land of Israel.

Jews think about this story a lot. The journey from slavery to freedom has made them what they are.

Inside a Jewish home

The home is the most important place for Jews to practice their religion. Celebrations take place there, usually with special food. Part of being Jewish means learning about Judaism. Parents read Jewish stories to younger children and teach more difficult writings to older children. Often families discuss Jewish ideas at mealtimes.

▲ A girl lighting Shabbat candles with her family.

Special Jewish objects

Jewish homes often have lots of Jewish books, pictures, and CDs, as well as objects used for **Shabbat** and festivals. There are usually candlesticks, a goblet and a cover for special bread.

The mezuzah

On the door frames of Jewish homes hangs a small box called a **mezuzah**, which contains an extract from the Torah called the **Shema**. This is part of one of the most important Jewish prayers. It tells Jews that there is only one God. Seeing the mezuzah reminds Jews to obey God's commandments.

▲ Many Jews touch the mezuzah when going into or out of buildings, including their homes.

Food

The **Torah**, meaning "teaching," is the most important part of the **scriptures**. One of the many things it teaches is what Jews may not eat—for example, pork. Food that Jews may eat is called "**Kasher**" (or "Kosher"). There are special rules about how to kill animals for food in a way that causes the animal the least pain.

Make a mezuzah

You will need: empty, clean glue stick tube with lid • 1 sheet white paper • 1 sheet construction paper • felt-tip pens • glue • poster putty

1 Cut the white paper into a 3 x 3 inch (8 x 8 cm) square. Write a quotation or saying on it that means a lot to you. Roll it up and place it inside the empty glue tube. Put the lid on.

2 Cut the construction paper into a 3 x 3 inch (8 x 8 cm) square. Draw a symbol on it to represent your home or school. You can color the symbol using the felt-tip pens if you want.

3 Glue or tape the construction paper around the tube, overlapping the edges. Use poster putty to attach your finished mezuzah to a door frame.

9

The day of rest

The most important day in the Jewish week lasts from sunset on Friday to sunset on Saturday. It is called Shabbat, which means "resting." Jews spend Shabbat with their family and community. It is a peaceful day, with no work. It begins when the mother of a Jewish family lights candles as a symbol of warmth and holiness.

The evening meal

Everyone wishes each other "Shabbat **Shalom**!" meaning "Sabbath peace." Parents give their children a blessing and may also say some personal words to each of them. The Kiddush, a blessing with wine or grape juice, is sung to bring in the holiness of Shabbat. The meal starts with breaking bread. There are two loaves as a reminder that, when they were in the wilderness, the ancient Jews had to gather two amounts of food every Friday— one for Friday itself and one for Shabbat.

◄ A father making kiddush with his family.

The next day

In **synagogue** on Shabbat morning, there is a reading from the Torah, followed by a talk about it. Shabbat afternoon is a quiet and personal time. When Shabbat is over, the family says goodbye to Shabbat by making **havdalah**. This ceremony marks the difference between the holy day and the working week. The family members wish each other "A good week!"

▲ A family making havdalah, with wine, a braided candle, and sweet-smelling spices.

Peace song

One of the many Jewish songs welcoming a spirit of peace into the home and heart says:
"Peace to you, messengers of the One on high, from the ruler who rules over all rulers, the Holy One! Come in peace... Bless me with peace... Leave in peace..."

Make a bread cover for a special meal

You will need: scratch paper • pencil • 10 in. x 7 in. (25 cm x 18 cm) white or light-colored cloth napkin • colored felt-tip pens • different-colored pencils • 1 yard (1 m) braid trim or beads • needle and white thread

1 Sketch and color in the design of your bread cloth on the paper. You could copy the design here, or draw an image showing a happy and peaceful time.

2 Copy your design carefully onto the center of the cloth using felt-tip pens. Leave it to dry.

3 To finish off, sew the trim or beads neatly around all four edges. Leave a 1 in. (3 cm) margin.

The cycle of Jewish life

As in all religious traditions, the stages in a Jewish person's life, such as birth, marriage, and death, are marked by certain rituals and ceremonies. These occasions remind Jews of God and the importance of obeying his laws.

Birth

Babies are welcomed not only for themselves, but also because they are part of the Jewish tradition that goes back 4,000 years. When a boy is born, there is a ceremony called **Brit Milah**, which shows that he is part of the **covenant**. Many families and communities have ceremonies for girls, as well. At these events, the baby's Hebrew name is announced, which might be different from the child's "everyday" name.

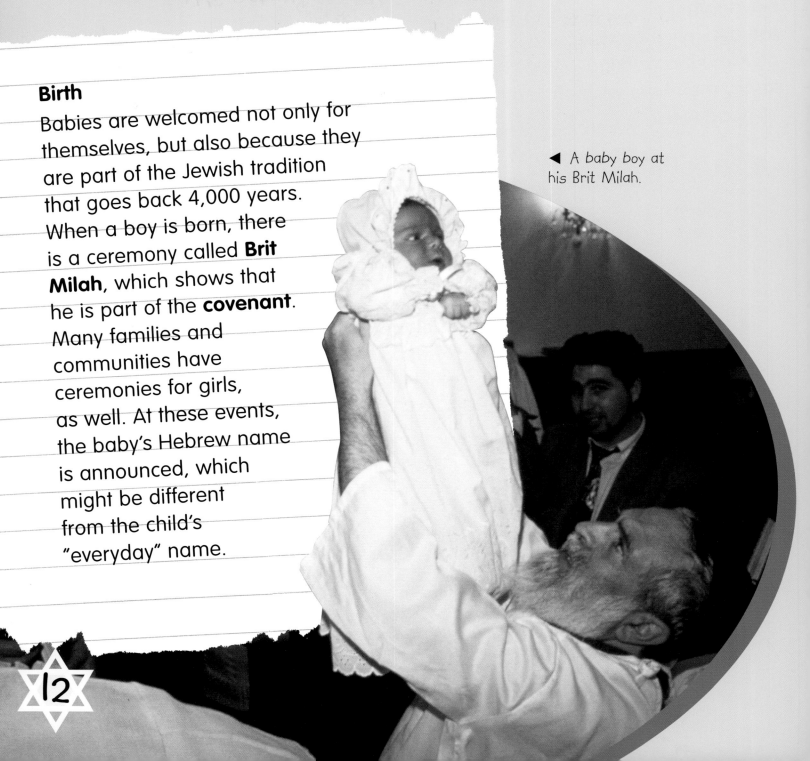

◀ A baby boy at his Brit Milah.

Growing up

At the age of 13, a Jewish boy counts as a man. He must start keeping the **mitzvot** for himself. He is called **Bar Mitzvah** (Son of the Commandment). To mark this time, he is usually called to read from the Torah in the synagogue. There is also a family or community party. Traditionally, a girl counts as a woman at the age of 12 and must start keeping the mitzvot for herself. She is called **Bat Mitzvah** (Daughter of the Commandment).

▲ This girl and her friends are lighting 12 candles for her Bat Mitzvah.

▶ Jewish weddings take place under a canopy called a huppah, which is a symbol of the bride and groom's new home.

Weddings

At a Jewish wedding, the bride points the index finger of her right hand, and the groom places a ring on it. Some brides also give their husband a ring. Under the huppah, the couple share wine as a symbol of joy and God's goodness. The marriage agreement is signed by witnesses and then kept by the bride as proof of the marriage. At the end of the ceremony, the groom breaks a wine glass under his foot to symbolize the fragile nature of human life.

Funerals

When a Jew dies, the funeral takes place as soon as possible so that family and friends can begin to mourn. In the first week, the family stays at home out of respect for the dead and to come to terms with their feelings. Relatives and friends keep them company. After a week, normal life continues, but the family does not go to any parties for 30 days.

13

Festivals and traditions

Some Jewish festivals are celebratory and happy, whereas others are quieter and encourage Jews to think about their past and traditions. There are five main festivals: Pesah, or Passover, celebrates the journey to freedom from slavery. Shavuot remembers when Moses received the Torah. Sukkot, in the fall, is a time when Jews eat their meals in temporary shelters, as the early Jews did in the wilderness. Rosh Hashanah celebrates the Jewish New Year and is followed by a festival called Yom Kippur. Jews do not work during any of these festivals.

▼ This man is blowing a ram's horn in the days leading up to Rosh Hashanah.

New Year

Rosh Hashanah comes in the fall. It is a time for Jews to look back on the year, to think about what they have done wrong or anyone they have hurt, and to try to put things right. They also look forward to the coming year, when they will try to be better. At Rosh Hashanah time, a ram's horn is blown, like a wake-up call.

Yom Kippur falls on the tenth day of the year and is linked to Rosh Hashanah. It is a time to confess any wrongdoings to God. To show that they are sorry, Jews do not eat or drink for 25 hours, unless they are very young or ill.

Passover

Passover comes in the spring. On the first evening of Passover, Jews have a meal, called seder, at home. They tell the story of how God set the Jewish nation free and sing songs. They act out parts of the story and eat symbolic foods. Yeast-free bread, called matzah, is eaten because the Jews left Egypt suddenly and didn't have time to let their bread rise. Bitter herbs stand for the bitterness of slavery. A sweet paste, called haroset, looks like the cement that the Jewish slaves used for building. The seder ends with hope for freedom for everyone.

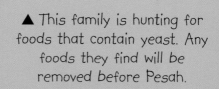

▲ This family is hunting for foods that contain yeast. Any foods they find will be removed before Pesah.

Recipe for haroset

You will need: 1 apple • knife • grater • bowl • pinch of cinnamon • ½ cup (50 g) chopped or ground nuts • 1 tablespoon grape juice • honey, to taste • spoon

1 Ask an adult to core, peel, and quarter the apple. Now grate it into a bowl.

2 Add all the other ingredients. Mix them together well. Leave to stand.

Shavuot

Shavuot, in the summer, celebrates the time that God gave the Torah to Moses. Nowadays on Shavuot, some Jews like to stay awake all night to receive the Torah again in their hearts.

15

Inside a synagogue

A synagogue is a community center for Jews. They go there to study and pray, to plan activities and hold celebrations. In traditional synagogues, men and women sit separately. In some synagogues, the men and women sit together.

The Ark

The main part of a synagogue is the Ark. This is the cupboard where the Torah scrolls are kept. It is often on the wall of the synagogue that points toward Jerusalem, in Israel. In North America and Europe, this is the southeastern wall. Above the Ark hangs a lamp that never goes out. It is a symbol of the Torah never dying and of God being eternal.

◀ The Ark in a Polish synagogue that is hundreds of years old.

Reading the Torah

When it is time to read the Torah, the Torah scroll is taken out of the Ark. People sing as it is carried around the synagogue and turn to follow it with their eyes. When it passes, they bow toward it to show respect and love. The Torah is read from a raised table or platform near the center or front of the room. Seating in the synagogue is usually arranged around three sides of the platform.

▲ These children are looking closely at a rolled-out Torah.

◀ A community party held at a synagogue.

The Torah scrolls

The Torah is handwritten on parchment scrolls. It is a skilled job, done by a specialist. It can take a whole year to write a full Torah. The scrolls are so precious that they must not be touched by hand. To avoid touching them, when someone reads from the Torah, they use a special silver pointer, called a yad.

17

Jewish community leaders

ost synagogues have a **rabbi**, who is a teacher and
preacher. In traditional synagogues, rabbis are men.
In other synagogues, rabbis may be men or women.
The rabbi teaches both adults and children how to study the
Torah. Some synagogues also have a youth leader, who runs
Jewish activities, sleepovers, and youth camps.

▼ This boy is reading from
the Torah. An adult guides
him as he reads.

Boards

Most synagogues have a board. The board members decide on all kinds of things, such as which charities to give the collections to, who will be in charge of decorating the **sukkah**, and who will be their rabbi. All adult members of the synagogue can vote for board members. Children do not have a vote, but in some synagogues a teenage boy and girl sit on board and give their opinions.

▶ A youth leader playing the guitar in a song session.

The hazzan

Many synagogues have a hazzan. The hazzan leads the singing of the prayers and also sings some solo parts. The Torah is chanted in a traditional way and the hazzan often teaches people how this is done so that they can chant, too.

Other important people

Many Jews help out in the synagogue, without it being their actual job. Members of the board and of the Hevrah Kadishah are all volunteers. Other volunteers also do jobs in the community, including visiting the sick, cooking community meals, or raising money for charity.

Hevrah Kadishah

Many Jewish communities have a Hevrah Kadishah, or Holy Society, who prepare the body of someone who has died for the funeral—men for the men, and women for the women. They think of it as holy work and do not expect thanks.

19

The Torah

The Torah is read aloud on Shabbat and festivals, and is also read twice during the week. It is the most important part of Jewish tradition. It contains stories and poems, as well as laws for living. Jews discuss, and sometimes argue about, what it means. Over many generations, Jews' ideas about the Torah have been written down so that each generation knows about the opinions of the ones in the past. It is like a chain of tradition.

Precious scroll

The Torah scroll is very precious and is always treated with care and devotion. Jews show their love and respect for the Torah in many ways. For example, when a Torah scroll eventually gets faded and worn out, it is not thrown away, but buried instead.

▲ Reading the Torah in a women's prayer group.

Forbidden text

Over 2,000 years ago, the Romans occupied the Land of Israel. They knew how much the Torah meant to the Jewish people, and they passed a law forbidding Jews to study it. They hoped it would make Judaism die out. A rabbi named Akiva, who lived at that time, told a story about a fox and a fish. In the story, the fox stands for the Romans and the fish for the Jews. The rabbi used the story to show the Jews that although it was hard to stay with the Torah (represented by the water), it was impossible to live without it.

▲ Dressing the Torah scroll again, after it has been read.

▶ A **Sefardi**-style Torah scroll, in a decorative cylinder case.

The fox and the fish

A fish was swimming happily in a stream, when along came a fox. He saw the fish and thought, "Mmm! That fish looks tasty!" So he called to her, "That stream looks so cold and dark. Up here, it's warm and bright. Why don't you jump out?" The fish knew at once that this was a trick and that she could never survive out of the water. She said to the fox, "I'm used to this stream and I need it to live. It may be hard to live IN the water, but it would be even harder for me to live OUTSIDE the water."

21

Important people

At all times in Jewish history, there have been men, women, and children who have inspired or encouraged Jews. These people have acted as good models for how to behave.

The story of Ester

Long ago, the king of Persia chose Ester as his wife—but no one in the palace knew she was Jewish. Ester's Jewish uncle, Mordechai, refused to bow down to one of the king's ministers. The minster was very angry and took revenge by plotting to kill all the Jews. Ester risked her life by appearing in the king's court to show her husband what his minister was really like. The king let the Jews defend themselves, and they were saved. Mordechai said that every year Jews should celebrate being saved by taking gifts of food to each other and giving money to the poor.

The first Hebrews

Abraham and Sarah lived about 4,000 years ago, in a place where people believed in many gods and worshipped idols. The Torah says that God spoke to Abraham and said: "Go to yourself—from your country, your community, and your parents' house to a land that I will show you. I will make you into a great people and I will bless you…and you will be a blessing." So they traveled a long way to the land that would be called "Israel". The people who made this journey were the first Hebrews. Jews call Abraham and Sarah the "father" and "mother" of the Jewish people.

▶ The Purim festival, when people dress up, comes from the Ester story.

Hannah Senesh

Hannah Senesh, born in Hungary in 1921, believed that the land of Israel was the home of the Jewish people and, at age 18, she settled there. When it became known that the Nazis were killing millions of Jews, she volunteered to parachute into Hungary to collect information and try to rescue Jews. Although the Nazis captured and tortured her, she never surrendered or betrayed her comrades. She was executed by the Nazis in 1944, at the age of 23.

▲ A photograph of Hannah Senesh.

Yitzhak Rabin

Yitzhak Rabin was born in Israel in 1922. A farmer, then a soldier, he twice became Prime Minister and signed peace agreements with the Palestinians. He won the Nobel Peace Prize in 1994. However, some people thought that making peace would make Israel unsafe and they tried to stop him. In 1995, while he was leaving a peace rally, he was shot and killed.

▶ A graffiti wall of remembrance at the place where Yitzhak Rabin was shot and died.

23

Israel

The Torah says that God promised Israel to the Jewish people. It was the first place in which they settled over 3,000 years ago. Most Jews believe that Israel is their homeland. Many countries have conquered Israel, and twice the Jews have been driven out—the last time by the Romans, 2,000 years ago. Wherever Jews have been, they have prayed for Israel.

Jerusalem

David, the best-loved king of ancient Israel, made Jerusalem its capital and chose the city as the site for a national temple. Today, Jerusalem remains the capital of modern Israel. Around the world, Jews turn toward Jerusalem when they pray.

▼ A town on a hill near Jerusalem.

24

The Western Wall

In ancient times, the temple was on a hill with a wall around it. The Romans destroyed most of the city of Jerusalem, including the temple. All that remains is the western part of the wall around the hill. Jews go there to pray, either alone or in groups.

▲ Men and women pray separately at the Western Wall.

◄ A car from one of the trains used by the Nazis to take away the Jews. It is now at Yad V'Shem.

The return to Israel

About 120 years ago, Jews from Europe started to return to Israel and, in 1948, Israel became an independent country. Many Jews who live outside Israel visit the country, and spend time at ancient sites, such as the Western Wall, and modern ones, including Yad V'Shem.

Holocaust memorial

Yad V'Shem is a memorial in Jerusalem to the Jews killed by the Nazis. It also has a Holocaust museum and database. There are many sculptures and monuments in the grounds of Yad V'Shem. People go there to study the history of the Holocaust and to think about it.

Judaism and the world today

Jews have lived outside Israel for 2,000 years, and during that time there have been Jewish communities in almost every country of the world. These communities have taken on the culture of the places in which they lived. For example, Jews in France speak French, Indian-Jewish women wear saris, and Mexican Jews eat Mexican food.

Two traditions

The Jewish communities that developed in northern Europe are called **Ashkenazi**. The Jewish communities that developed in southern Europe and the Middle East are called Serfardi. There are some differences between Ashkenazi and Sefardi Jews, in their styles of worship and in other customs, such as the kinds of food they eat and the ways they pronounce Hebrew.

▶ Jews at a market in Be'er Sheva, in the south of Israel.

Practicing today

Today, some Jewish communities have changed certain Jewish customs and styles of worship, or have decided not to keep them. They feel that, because the world is changing, some parts of Judaism should change, too. Other Jews believe that Judaism is an eternal religion and should never change, no matter how much life changes. Many communities combine Jewish traditions with modern ways. No matter what they feel about Jewish traditions, Jews play their part in the society in which they live.

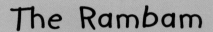

▲ Jews at a rally for peace in London, England.

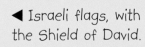

◀ Israeli flags, with the Shield of David.

The Rambam

Giving to charity remains an important Jewish custom. A famous Spanish-Jewish teacher called the Rambam spoke about how important it is to do good for someone else and to do it well. He imagined a ladder with different steps that explained the best way to give (see page 29).

27

Activity Make a ladder of charity

You will need:

• 4 sheets of 8 ½ x 11 inch (21 x 30 cm) poster paper • pencil • ruler • scissors • black and colored felt-tip pens • glue stick • sponge • poster paints • gold metallic pen • push pins or poster putty

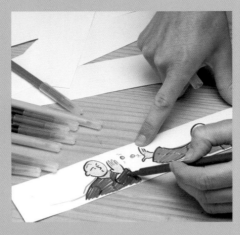

1 Measure and cut the card into 14 strips, 2 in. x 11 in. (5 cm x 30 cm) wide. Eight of the strips will be the rungs of the ladder. The other six will be used for the two posts. (You will have two pieces left over.)

2 On one horizontal strip, draw and color in a scene to represent the bottom rung of the ladder (see 'The ladder' opposite). Leave a 2-inch (5 cm) margin at each end. Repeat for the other seven rungs of the ladder.

3 Glue three of the leftover strips together to make a longer strip, overlapping by about ½ inch (1 cm). This will form one of the posts of the ladder. Repeat with three more strips for the other post.

4 Now create the ladder shape with the two posts and the eight rungs. Check that the steps are in the right order and that there are about 2 inches (5 cm) between each rung. Use one of the leftover strips as a guide.

28

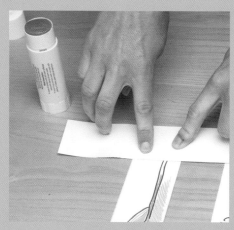

5 Position the posts on top of the rungs, overlapping them by about ½ inch (1 cm). Glue the rungs to the backs of the posts. Leave them to dry.

6 On one of the leftover strips of poster paper, draw two triangles to create a Star of David. Carefully cut out the shape to make a template.

7 Decorate the posts by sponging paint over your star-shaped template using different colors. If you like, you could outline each star with a black or gold pen when the paint is dry.

8 Use push pins or poster putty to attach your ladder of charity to a door or wall.

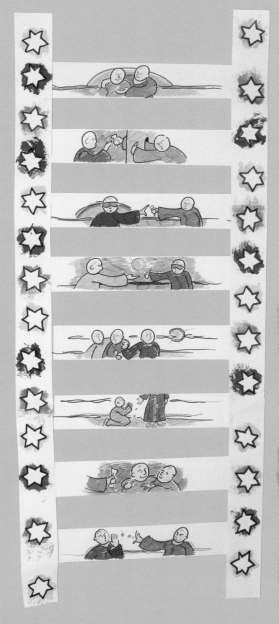

The ladder

Best of all...
Lending someone money or finding them work so they never need charity again.
Is better than...
Giving charity, without knowing who you give it to and without them knowing that it comes from you.
Is better than...
Giving charity, knowing who you give it to but without them knowing that it comes from you.
Is better than...
Giving charity, without knowing who you give it to but with them knowing that it comes from you.
Is better than...
Giving charity before being asked.
Is better than...
Giving charity after being asked.
Is better than...
Giving less charity than you should, but nicely.
Is better than...
Giving charity, but in a miserable way.

29

Glossary

Ashkenazi Jews Jews who are part of the Jewish community in or from northern Europe.

Bar Mitzvah A title, meaning "Son of the Commandment," given to a boy when he reaches the age of 13 and is considered a man. It is also the name of the ceremony that marks this occasion.

Bat Mitzvah A title that means "Daughter of the Commandment" and is the title given to a Jewish girl when she turns 12 years old and is thought of as an adult. As with Bar Mitzvah, it is also used as the name of the ceremony.

Brit Milah A special ceremony held for a baby boy to show that he is part of the promise Jewish people believe God made with them.

covenant The belief that God has promised to protect and help the Jewish people in return for obeying his religious laws. This promise between God and the Jewish people is also known as a "brit."

havdalah A special ceremony, using wine, sweet spices, and a candle, which marks the end of Shabbat and other festivals.

Hebrews The very first name given to the Jewish people. Hebrew is also the language used in Israel. Jewish holy writings and prayers are written in Hebrew.

Israelites The name by which the Jewish people were known after they were called Hebrews, but before they were called Jews.

Jerusalem The most holy city of Judaism, where many sacred buildings and places are found. It is also where the government of Israel is located.

kasher (or kosher) Food that is kasher has been prepared according to Jewish rules. This means that Jews are allowed to eat it.

mezuzah A small box that hangs on the door frame of a Jewish house. Jews often touch the mezuzah on their way in and out of their home. It reminds them to obey God's commandments.

Middle East A region of the world that includes places such as Israel, Egypt, and Jordan.

mitzvot The religious rules that Jews follow.

rabbi A Jewish teacher and preacher.

scriptures All the holy writings of a religion. Jewish scriptures include the Torah, as well as other writings.

Sefardi Jews Jews who are part of the Jewish communities in or from southern Europe and the Middle East.

Shabbat The Jewish holy day of rest, which begins at sunset each Friday and ends at sunset each Saturday. Shabbat is usually reserved for family activities and prayer.

Shalom The Hebrew word for "peace." It is used as a greeting and also to say hello and goodbye. "Shabbat shalom" means "Sabbath peace" and is said on Shabbat.

Shema A part of the Torah. Each mezuzah contains the Shema, written out on a piece of parchment.

sukkah An outdoor shelter that is decorated for the Jewish harvest festival of Sukkot.

synagogue A house of worship where Jews go to pray, study, and celebrate their religion.

Ten Sayings Ten important rules which were given to God by Moses and which tell Jews how they should live and behave.

Torah The most important part of the Jewish scriptures, chanted from a scroll.

Index

Notes for parents and teachers

This book is an accessible introduction to the beliefs and practices of the Jewish faith. It does not aim to be a comprehensive guide, but gives plenty of opportunity for additional activities and study.

Visiting a synagogue

Visiting a synagogue provides a useful insight into Jewish practice in the community. When making arrangements beforehand, it is a good idea to ask if a Torah scroll can be brought out and opened. Touching the parchment with bare hands is not allowed. Photography is usually acceptable, but it is good to ask permission first. It is sensitive if males and females dress modestly. Men and boys may be asked to wear a head covering: this can be a hat or cap of their choosing, but synagogues also provide yarmulkes (skullcaps).

Useful websites

www.akhlah.com
Akhlah, the "Jewish Children's Learning Network," has lots of short, kid-friendly articles about important aspects of Judaism on its site.

www.jewfaq.org
"Judaism 101" is an online encyclopedia containing articles on all aspects of Judaism.

www.j.co.il
Jewish Education & Entertainment contains some interactive games and links to information on Bar and Bat Mitzvahs.

Activities for children

Judaism originated in the Middle East, in areas that include present-day Israel and Egypt. Look at a map of this part of the world and have the children identify some important cities and geographical features such as rivers and bodies of water. What kind of climate do these areas have? Identify areas of desert and mountains on the map. Ask the children what they think it would have been like to live in this part of the world in the time of Abraham and Sarah and other early Jews.

Jews face in the direction of the holy city of Jerusalem when they pray. With the help of a globe or world map and a compass if necessary, find out where Jerusalem lies in relation to where you are now.

Look at the descriptions of Jewish festivals on pages 14–15. Ask the children to choose one of these festivals and then use books or the Internet to find out more about it: when is it celebrated? Where do people celebrate it? What do they wear? Are there any special objects used in the celebration? Have the children draw or paint a picture or make a diorama depicting the festival and then explain it to the rest of the group.